Born to be Wild
Little Giraffes

D1270389

Christian Marie

Words that appear in the glossary are printed in
boldface type the first time they occur in the text.

 **Gareth Stevens**
Publishing

The Land of Giants

The big day has arrived. In a quiet place on Africa's large **savanna**, a mother giraffe is ready for the birth of her new baby. A baby giraffe arrives by dropping out of its mother's body and landing in the soft grass of the savanna. The mother immediately begins licking her baby to urge it to stand. A newborn giraffe has trouble standing on its long, fragile legs. The little giraffe will not be able to take its first steps for a few hours.

A mother giraffe carries her unborn baby inside her body for sixteen months. Most baby giraffes are born in spring, when there is plenty of grass for them to eat.

What do you think ?

How can a mother giraffe **graze** peacefully without having to keep a close eye on her baby?

a) She leaves her baby near young giraffes that are closely guarded by other female giraffes.

b) She leads her baby to a quiet place and lets it know it should not move from that spot.

c) She leaves her baby with its father.

A mother giraffe can graze peacefully because she leaves her baby near young giraffes that are closely guarded by other female giraffes.

For the first few days after giving birth, a mother giraffe, which is called a cow, stays near her baby, or calf. She will not leave her calf alone and defenseless. After three or four weeks, she leads the calf toward the other little giraffes in the **herd**. One or two other mother giraffes keep an eye on all the calves, just like in a day care center! Because they live in a herd, little giraffes can play together, and their mothers can eat undisturbed.

A giraffe calf looks a lot like its mother. Two tufts of soft black hair grow at the ends of a calf's small horns. The hair will become coarser as the calf's horns grow larger.

At birth, a giraffe calf weighs about 130 pounds (60 kilograms), as much as a human adult female. A calf is about 6 feet (2 meters) tall — almost four times more than a human newborn baby.

A young giraffe grows very fast — as much as 4 inches (10 centimeters) a month during its first year. The little giraffe will soon be a giant, just like its mom!

A Giraffe's L-O-N-G Neck

Young giraffes grow quickly, developing long legs and long necks. When they are adults, some giraffes stand more than 16 feet (5 m) tall — twice the height of an elephant. A giraffe cannot easily move through the savanna without being seen. Although the large, dark brown spots on its coat help a giraffe hide among the trees, it can still be recognized from far away.

What do you think?

Why does a giraffe have such a long neck?

a) to make it look different from other animals

b) to give it a good view of the savanna

c) to help it feed on the tops of trees and spot danger more easily

The neck of an adult giraffe can measure up to 84 inches (213 cm) long. It has seven **cervical vertebrae**, each one measuring about 12 inches (30 cm) long. Humans also have seven vertebrae in their necks, but human vertebrae are much shorter.

A giraffe's long neck helps it feed on the tops of trees and spot danger more easily.

The front legs of a giraffe are a little longer than its back legs, causing its body to slope backwards. Compared to its long legs, a giraffe's body is short. Its neck, however, is very long and allows a giraffe to eat leaves from the tops of trees. Few other animals can reach food this high. Having such a long neck also helps a giraffe keep an eye on its surroundings.

A giraffe's tail bends and moves easily. It has a long, thick tuft of black hair at the tip.

A giraffe's coat is covered with irregular spots. No two coats are alike, so each giraffe is one of a kind!

When giraffes move slowly, they bend their knees slightly, which makes the animals look stiff. As they walk, giraffes move their right legs forward, at the same time, and then move their left legs.

Giraffes can run up to 37 miles (60 kilometers) per hour. Although they are moving quickly, giraffes look graceful when they gallop. They swing their back legs forward, at the same time, and then move their front legs. Their long necks sway back and forth, which helps the animals keep their balance.

Good Food for Growing Giraffes

A little giraffe will drink milk from its mother's body for about one year. When a calf is four weeks old, it also starts to eat the same foods as the adults. During the cooler parts of the day — in the morning, in the evening, or at night — a calf grazes on the leaves of small bushes and trees. It also eats the flowers, fruits, and grasses of the savanna. A young giraffe's black tongue is rough and stretches to reach the best buds.

For its first few months of life, a calf's main food is its mother's milk. By the time it is six months old, a calf will mainly eat plants, but it will also drink milk for several more months.

What do you think ?

Why do giraffes go several days without drinking water?

a) Their food provides giraffes with enough water.

b) Giraffes do not like to drink.

c) A giraffe's long legs make bending down to drink painful.

Giraffes go several days without drinking water because their food provides enough water.

A giraffe's main activity is eating. An adult giraffe can eat up to 145 pounds (65 kg) of food a day. **Acacia** is a giraffe's favorite meal. The leaves of the acacia tree are filled with water, so when a giraffe eats acacia leaves, it does not need to drink.

A giraffe is a **ruminant mammal**, which means its stomach has four separate chambers. A ruminant eats and swallows its food quickly, then brings the **cud**, or swallowed food, back up into its mouth and chews it again for a longer time. Finally, the food goes into another part of the stomach to be fully digested.

Bending down to drink is very difficult for giraffes. They have to spread their legs very far apart to reach the water.

When a young giraffe has all its teeth, it can imitate the adults as they search through leafy branches. Using their teeth, giraffes bite through leaves and skip the less tasty stalks.

A giraffe's head suits the way the animal feeds. Its slender and **tapered** shape helps the giraffe reach between branches. The long hairs covering its lips help a giraffe pick the best leaves — and know where the thorns are, too.

Staying Safe in the Savanna

The savanna is a dangerous place for a young giraffe. Lions, leopards, and hyenas are always on the **prowl**, looking for weak **prey** that is easy to catch. Young giraffes must always be guarded. When it is in the center of the herd, a little giraffe is well protected. All the female giraffes stand guard. If one of them senses danger, she alerts the rest of the group with a sudden swat of her tail.

What do you think?

Why does a giraffe drink water quickly?

a) because it does not know how to drink slowly

b) because it is in danger when it bends down to drink

c) because it does not want to share the water with the other giraffes

Giraffes have good eyesight. They can see small movements from more than one-half mile (1 km) away! The savanna is open **terrain**, and with their long necks, giraffes have a clear view all around them.

A giraffe drinks water quickly because it is in danger when it bends down to drink.

When a calf is in danger, a mother giraffe quickly steps in to help. Using her back hooves, she attacks the **predator** with a big kick. When a calf and its mother stop to drink, however, they are both in danger. With their legs spread wide and their bodies bent over, they will have trouble reacting quickly if they need to defend themselves against big cats or any other predators.

Giraffes can run fast across the savanna because the soil is very hard. With their thin legs, giraffes would have trouble running on soft ground.

Lions do not take chances against an adult giraffe's powerful hooves. A giraffe's hooves can crush a lion's head and sides. In open areas, big cats attack only young giraffes.

With its legs bent and spread apart, and its hooves digging into the mud, a giraffe is easy prey. It drinks quickly, often with another giraffe standing guard.

Little giraffes will lie down in the grass only under the watchful eyes of their mothers. Giraffes usually sleep standing up and do not sleep for more than a total of four or five hours a day.

Giraffe Families

Every day, a giraffe calf roams the savanna in search of food with its herd of females and other young giraffes. Sometimes, giraffes from another herd join their group. A herd can have up to fifteen giraffes.

When young male giraffes reach the age of three or four, they leave the herd, and at mating time, begin searching for female companions. Older males either live alone or in a group of all males.

Giraffes swing their long necks over the savanna's small trees. This movement helps them watch for danger at the same time that they are finding the most delicious acacia leaves.

What do you think?

Why do male giraffes fight with each other?

a) to decide who will mate with a female

b) to decide which is the most powerful male

c) to pass the time

Male giraffes fight to decide who will mate with a female.

Male giraffes are always ready to fight. First, they spread their legs to keep their balance. Then they wind their necks together and hit each other with their heads. Sometimes, a giraffe is injured by the other animal's pointed horns. When all the fighting is over, the strongest giraffe will be able to attract females for mating without competition from other males.

A little giraffe never knows its father. After mating, a male giraffe disappears into the savanna.

Male giraffes begin to fight each other when they are about three years of age.

Fighting among adult males is not usually dangerous, but after a few fights, the loser leaves the group and moves away.

Giraffes are mammals that, in the wild, live in the grassy African savanna. They live about twenty-five years in the wild and thirty-five years in captivity. They can weigh up to 4,000 pounds (1,800 kg).

Giraffes are related to the okapi — an African animal with a body shaped like a giraffe's but with a much shorter neck and legs that are striped like a zebra.

A giraffe has two short horns on its head. Each horn is covered with skin and hair.

A giraffe's coat has large, dark brown spots.

A giraffe has very good eyesight.

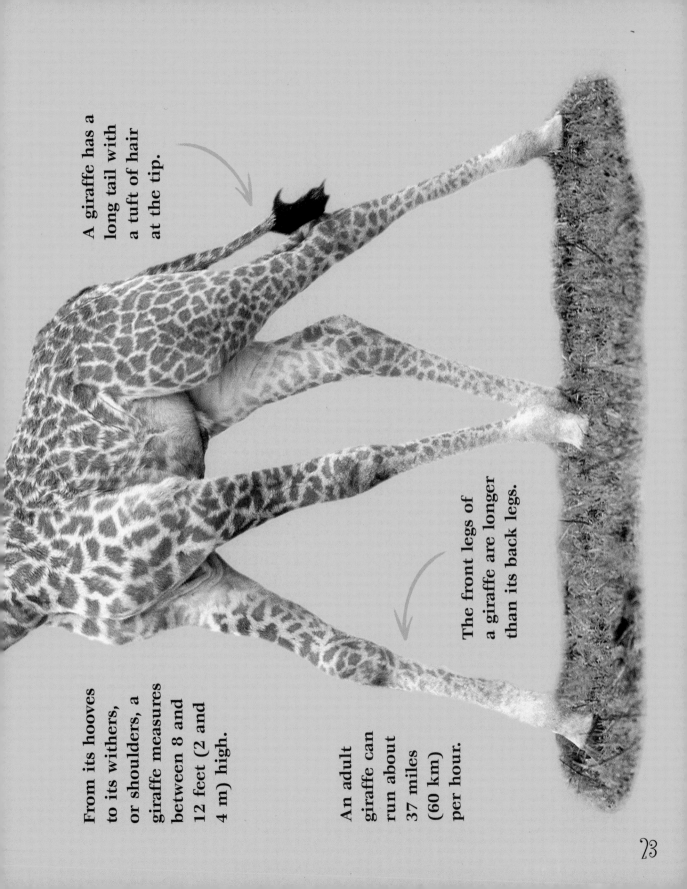

A giraffe has a long tail with a tuft of hair at the tip.

The front legs of a giraffe are longer than its back legs.

From its hooves to its withers, or shoulders, a giraffe measures between 8 and 12 feet (2 and 4 m) high.

An adult giraffe can run about 37 miles (60 km) per hour.

GLOSSARY

acacia — a small tree or shrub with feathery leaves and white or yellow flowers

cervical — related to the neck

cud — food that has been swallowed by an animal and brought up from the stomach to be chewed again

graze — feed on grass and other growing plants

herd — a group of one kind of animal that stays together

mammals — warm-blooded animals that have backbones, give birth to live babies, feed their young with milk from the mother's body, and have skin that is usually covered with hair or fur

predator — an animal that kills other animals for food

prey — animals that are hunted and killed by a predator

prowl — move about secretly and quietly in search of prey

ruminant — related to an animal that chews cud; an animal that is a ruminant mammal

savanna — a large, flat area of grassland with scattered trees, found in warm parts of the world

tapered — gradually becoming narrower or thinner

terrain — an area of land and its physical features

vertebrae — the separate bones that form a spine, or backbone

Please visit our web site at: www.garethstevens.com
For a free color catalog describing Gareth Stevens Publishing's list of high-quality books and multimedia programs, call 1-800-542-2595 (USA) or 1-800-387-3178 (Canada). Gareth Stevens Publishing's fax: 1-877-542-2596

Library of Congress Cataloging-in-Publication Data

Marie, Christian.
   [Petite girafe. English]
   Little giraffes / Christian Marie. — North American ed.
     p. cm. — (Born to be wild)
     ISBN-10: 0-8368-4436-X   ISBN-13: 978-0-8368-4436-8 (lib. bdg.)
    1. Giraffe—Infancy—Juvenile literature. I. Title. II. Series.
QL737.U56M35513   2005
599.638'139—dc22
                            2004059716

This North American edition first published in 2005 by
Gareth Stevens Publishing
A Weekly Reader Company
1 Reader's Digest Rd.
Pleasantville, NY 10570-7000 USA

This U.S. edition copyright © 2005 by Gareth Stevens, Inc.

Original edition copyright © 2001 by Mango Jeunesse.
First published in 2001 as *La petite girafe* by Mango Jeunesse, an imprint of Editions Mango, Paris, France.
Picture Credits [top = t, bottom = b, left = l, right = r]
Bios: M. and C. Denis-Huot title page, 21, 22–23; N. Granier 17(t). Colibri: A. M. Loubsens cover, 4, 16, 22; D. Hautoin 17(r). Jacana: M. Denis-Huot 5(r), 10, 13(r); S. Corolier 18; P. Wild 20(l). Phone: J-M Labat back cover, 2, 8(both), 15, 17(l); Ferrerro/Labat 5(l), 9(both), 11, 19, 20(r); Ch. Courteau 12. Sunset: G. Laez 3, 13(l), 14; Horizon vision 6, 7.

English translation: Pat Lantier
Gareth Stevens editor: Barbara Kiely Miller
Gareth Stevens art direction: Tammy West

Printed in the United States of America

2 3 4 5 6 7 8 9 09 08